For Hannah, Nathan, and Ryan
–V. M.

For Lydia and Isaac
–B. W.

# Dewey
## There's a Cat in the Library!

by Vicki Myron and Bret Witter

illustrated by Steve James

**LB**

Little, Brown and Company

New York   Boston

Every night, people left books in the return box of the library in the small town of Spencer, Iowa. Funny books, big books, truck books, pig books—they left them all.

But one night,

on the coldest night of the year,

someone left a strange surprise…

A tiny kitten.

When Vicki the librarian found him the next morning, the kitten was cold and scared and very, very dirty. Vicki took one look and decided to give him a warm bath. The kitten went into the sink brown and crying, but he came out orange and purring.

"I'm going to keep you," said Vicki, who already loved him.

"We'll name you Dewey Readmore Books. You can live here and be our library cat."

But Dewey had no idea what it meant to be a library cat.
So he did what all kittens do—he played.

He lounged on the newspaper…

Rode the book cart…

And knocked pens to the floor.

He goofed around with Marty Mouse…

Snooped in every open drawer…

And always found at least one rubber band.

But what Dewey loved most of all was people.
Tall ones. Round ones. Quiet ones. Loud ones. The *little* ones, however, surprised him. And not always in a good way.

"Look, Nathan," said his mommy.

*"There's a cat in the library."*

Nathan bent down and said, "Hi, Hooey Doowey Yooks."

"No," said his sister, Hannah, "it's Dewey Readmore Books!"

Dewey squirmed. The boy was petting him in the wrong direction! Dewey loved to be petted, but he *hated* being petted in the wrong direction.

Dewey was licking his fur back into place when
he heard a strange noise.

"Waaaa!"

Dewey's ears perked up. He looked around.

"Waaaaaaaa!"

"Waaaaaaaaaaaa!"

Dewey sprang to attention
and crept *re-e-e-eally*
slowly toward the sound.

# Surprise!

The little people, Dewey discovered,
came in tiny sizes too!

And they loved to giggle.

And grab.

And pull.

And coo.

*Babies are wonderful,*
Dewey thought.
*Cute and SMELL-icious, too.*

A few days later, Dewey went exploring and discovered, in a secret room, the most exciting thing he had ever seen. Children's Story Hour!

*Wowzy whiskers, this looks fun*, Dewey thought, as he pushed into the room with his nose.

Someone shouted:

"There's a cat in the library!"

Dewey froze.

It was quiet for one minute.

Then everything went wild!

And the next thing Dewey knew,
he was being carried upside-down.

*Oh my*, Dewey thought, *what should I do now*?

Late that night, Dewey talked to his friend Marty Mouse.

*The library is a wonderful place,* Dewey said, *but I'm tired of being pulled and poked and carried upside-down. I'm not just a cat in a library, I'm a Library Cat. A library cat helps people, I think, and I'm ninety-two percent convinced that that's the reason I'm around.*

Marty Mouse didn't say anything.

*I'm gonna do it,* Dewey said. *I'm going to help people.* And he felt so happy that he threw Marty Mouse into the air, kicked him with his

The next morning, when the first people arrived,
Dewey was waiting to greet them right by the front door.

All morning, Dewey acted like a library cat.
He read with the mommies and grandmas...

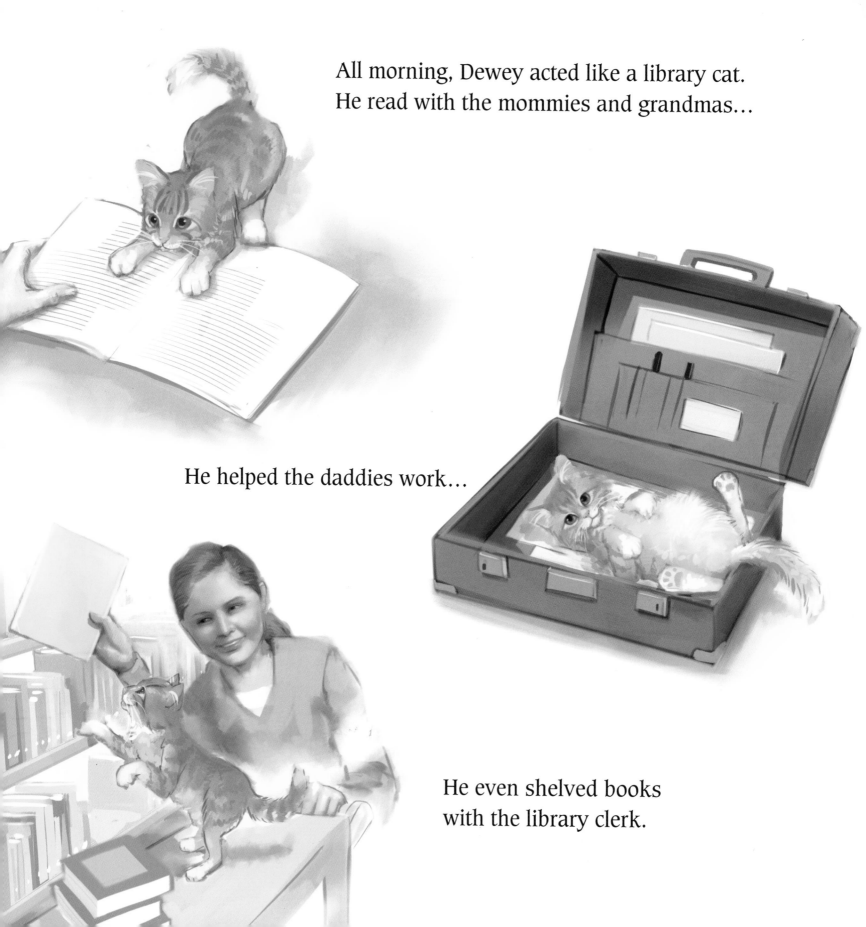

He helped the daddies work...

He even shelved books
with the library clerk.

When he saw little Nathan, he turned a circle and a half so the
boy could pet his back from his head down to his tail—the *right*
direction to pet a cat.

"I'm glad we're friends, De-woo-ley," Nathan said.

Dewey smiled at that.

By lunchtime Dewey was worn out.

So he found a good box.

First he put his front paws inside, then his belly.

He squished his back end down,

wiggled around

until he was all the way in…

and closed his eyes.

"There's an orange muffin in the library," a girl giggled.

But just as Dewey was about to drift off into sweet kitten dreams, he heard a heavy sigh. His eyes popped open, and he saw a girl on the other side of the library.

A sad little girl reading very quietly all by herself.

He climbed up close and stared at her.
She looked the other way.

He sniffed her hand.
She wouldn't play.

He knocked her mittens
to the floor.
She let them stay.

Then he saw her jacket and had his best idea yet....

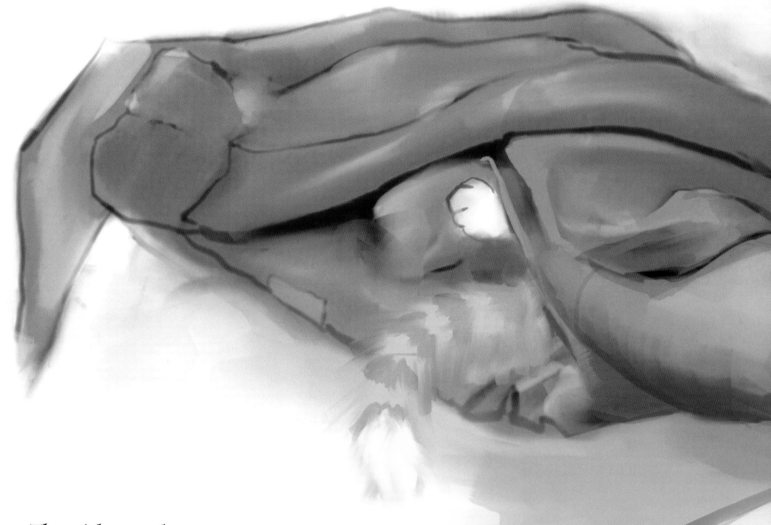

Silly always works!

I'll be a silly cat today!

The girl stared at Dewey.

"You look like a fuzzy hotdog in a purple bun," she said.

And then she surprised him.

She laughed right out loud.

"I love you, Dewey Readmore Books," the girl whispered, as Dewey nestled into her lap and began to purr.

*This is it*, Dewey thought.
*I'm a REAL library cat, and it feels great.*

No, it felt better than great.
It felt...*purr-fect!*